WALKING SCARECROW

Walking Scarecrow

The Poems of Pineshadow

by Mark Tate

Blue Light Press ❖ 1st World Publishing

San Francisco ❖ Fairfield ❖ Delhi

Winner of the Blue Light Book Award

Walking Scarecrow
The Poems of Pineshadow
Copyright ©2024 by Mark Tate

All rights reserved. Printed in the United States of America. No part of this book may be used or reproduced in any manner whatsoever without written permission except in the case of brief quotations embodied in critical articles and reviews. For information contact:

1st World Library
PO Box 2211
Fairfield, IA 52556
www.1stworldpublishing.com

Blue Light Press
www.bluelightpress.com
bluelightpress@aol.com

Book & Cover Design
Melanie Gendron
melaniegendron999@gmail.com

Cover Photo
Mark Tate

Author Photo
Jim Phillips

First Edition

Library of Congress Cataloging-in-Publication Data

ISBN: 978-1-4218-3554-9

In memory of

Ryu Nakazawa

March 18, 1938 to April 4, 2020

It walked with me

As I walked,

    The scarecrow in the distance.
                      – Sanin

The bright moon:

On the tatami

    The shadow of the pine-tree.
                      – Kikaku

walking on walking,
                under foot   earth turns.
                      – Gary Snyder

Contents

Preface xi

POEMS AFTER HANSHAN

Dragonfly and Woodcutter 1
Before the Banquet 2
Not Given Much Thought 3
Red Stems of the Japanese Maples 4
As He Lay in Bed, His Wife – 5
Polistinae 6
Philosopher and Perch 7
Figure a Way to Save the World 8
Too Hot or Too Cold 9
Along the Narrow Road 10
The Four Directions 11
Dream 12
Bees in the Shirley Poppies 13
Inheritance 14
Accommodations 15
Tahlequah 16
The Many Birds 17
Walking for What Ails Us 18
Strangers 19
Tea 20

Whispers	21
Memory of Japan	22
Moments	23
Light and Dark	24
Glorious Leader	25
Flowering Maple	26
Father	27
Seeing My Daughter	28
Wild Geese	29
Hawk and Dove	30
Correct Form	31
Ravens, Crows	32

Notes	33
Acknowledgments	35
About the Author	37

Preface

Some years ago, I began a hermitage. I had been helping my sisters take care of our parents, Mom with Alzheimer's and Dad with lymphoma. When they died, I needed a break. I had already reduced my work to part-time and was willing to let that go now as well. I wanted some time and space to think and feel, and I wanted to garden, to read, perhaps to resume writing. But there were others who called to me and concerns that I couldn't ignore. I had remarried and was living with my wife, Lori, at her mother's long-time Sonoma County property, which Shirley had named Pineshadow. Lori and I realized that my aging mother-in-law would need more care, as she was going blind and was in denial about her hearing loss.

My ex-wife, the mother of my son and daughter, and I had divorced long before. My son and daughter suffered the breakup of our marriage in radically different ways, and their health and place in society was an ever-present concern for both of us. Eventually, my former wife was diagnosed with ovarian cancer, and I was also concerned about her care. I took her to chemo appointments and sat with her. When she had enough energy, we would strategize about our daughter's addiction and about our son's stress, working together to parent our children the best we could.

Pineshadow, a two-acre property originally purchased by Shirley in the mid-seventies, is about five miles outside the city limits of Santa Rosa, California. Our sanctuary is shared with close to one hundred trees – pines, firs, oaks, madrones, and Japanese maples – and two cats who seem happy to follow us around. My wife was still working, so I became a house husband, caregiver, cat herder, and yardman. I scheduled my duties around four-mile morning walks on the gravel-covered lanes near the Laguna de Santa Rosa.

For a long time, I had wanted to re-read the classics of Asian literature in my home library and to find books mentioned by translators and editors that I had not yet read. I ordered *The Manyoshu*, *From the Country of Eight Islands*, *The Book of Song*, *Mirror for the Moon*, *An Anthology of Chinese Verse*, *Chiyo-ni: Woman Haiku Master*, and many others. I read to inform my writing, but also to test and confirm my sensibilities on how to live my life. As I read and re-read these thirty or forty books, representations of the broad Asian diaspora, I kept returning to Burton Watson's translation of the Tang poet Hanshan. And in my caretaker role, I enjoyed providing sustenance and comfort to Shirley.

Going in and out of Shirley's attached apartment one afternoon to check on her, I noticed that she held an oddly folded 4-inch square of newspaper up to the magnifying glasses she wore, and I thought it best if I began reading to her. Eventually, however, this practice had to change because Shirley would fall asleep in the middle of my reading of a news article or of an opinion piece, and Lori and I decided that I should try reading short poems to her. Shirley said she had never really "got what poets were saying," but that she was "game." I searched through books of haiku for what I thought she would enjoy. I hoped that the ancient poets would soothe Shirley as her world narrowed.

In R. H. Blyth's four-volume study of the art of haiku, I found in his chapter on Zen the haiku that I have used as an epigraph for this book. Blyth describes a "walking scarecrow" written by an obscure poet identified as Sanin. In the poem a scarecrow is personified by the walker – presumably an old man – who'd become a friend tramping with him. Each step shared between them constantly changes their perceptions, an appealing idea, a jaunting kind of companionship.

In Miyazawa Kenji's book *A Future of Ice*, his poem "November 3rd," in which the line "living in the shadow of pine trees in a field" tugged at my curious mind, reminding me that my mother-in-law's residence was named Pineshadow. Shirley explained that she had named her house after hearing of a neighborhood somewhere in Sonoma County with the same name. When I pressed her to tell me where I might find this area, she waved her hand, dismissing the question as insignificant – she'd forgotten.

Nevertheless, as I read Hanshan, known as Cold Mountain; and Bashō, a haiku master who adopted the name of a plant growing near his hut as a nom de plume; and other ancient poets who lived quiet lives, I felt I was on the right path. What began as a homage to Hanshan continued over several years as a dialogue with the reclusive poet of whom we know so little, and at the same time, I began to pay homage to the famed poet Li Po; to the haiku masters who had captivated my imagination; and to Zen poets such as Ikkyū Sōjun, whose irreverence and frankness I admired. I kept my Asian-inspired jottings in a box in my closet. I thought of these writings as divergences from the poetry I'd been writing since the early 1970s, and I adopted the name Pineshadow as my pseudonym. As I wrote, keeping in mind the ancient poets, I imagined that as Pineshadow I could have dialogues with these "scarecrows" walking with me in spirit.

Now an old man, I have gone through my writings and gathered some of them for this book, hoping that my work will move readers and spur them to revisit "the ancients" for inspiration. As I walk, I hear the crows in the pine trees. Come along with me!

– Mark Tate
October 2022, Sonoma County, California

POEMS AFTER HANSHAN

DRAGONFLY AND WOODCUTTER

As I walk in the heat of the olive orchard,
A dragonfly darts past me; I am pleased
With the afternoon sunlight streaming through
The field. My wife's shovel scrapes again;
She is planting in the garden boxes. A neighbor
And his son ring the gate bell, return a cooking dish.
I clap hands, calling the cats to come in from play.
Without envying the life or pursuits of others,
Thus blessed, we save a few dollars every month
For the woodcutter's arrival and his services.

BEFORE THE BANQUET

Preparing for the neighborhood banquet,
Readying the spring garden, finalizing
Changes to the fields, paths, and planters,
I find our "sleeping dogs," issues we should leave
For a later time – and under slate stones
At the new gate, thousands of teeming ants.
After days of weeding, our backs ache, and
We stretch to follow the unbridled birds afar.
Look: blooming poppies, roses, and elderberry.

NOT GIVEN MUCH THOUGHT

"Six polite arts of the Chinese gentleman:
Etiquette, music, archery, charioteering,
Calligraphy, and mathematics." Of course,
Charioteering is not taught at the university,
And etiquette has not been given much thought lately.
Are there still hermits in the remote mountains
Avoiding the politics of the grand capitol?
I recall the website 100,000 Poets. Surely
They've not holed up somewhere, obscured
From the reach of Our Glorious Leader! but rather
Developing our modern polite arts: music, dance,
Gallant athletic games, sanctuaries for endangered species,
Op/Ed conversation, and writing. Let us not forget
Iterations of poetry and jazz expand forever
Like the universe.

RED STEMS OF THE JAPANESE MAPLES

The tenuousness of life, like the red stems
Of the Japanese maple leaves, threads so easily
Severed. With age, do we have wisdom?
At least we recognize impermanence.
Your parents are gone, your physician retires,
Your family has spread far from town,
Friends and colleagues stop seeking you –
You have difficulty seeing, you complain that you
Cannot hear well, and your steps are halting.
As you sleep in your chair, the squirrels overrun
The bird feeders. Do you dream of flying?

AS HE LAY IN BED, HIS WIFE –

"This note is to let you know that after his visit
Yesterday, my husband came down with an illness
Called garden envy, and a touch of furniture envy
As well: 'How beautiful their house, like an article
In *Architectural Digest*,' he said. He lay down
To 'quiet the ills of his mind,' he said. I brought
Him tea and sat with him for a while. With guilt
For his own desires, he recounted your thoughts
Of letting your children put selection stickers
On the backs of the hand-made furniture.
'Glorious pieces of art,' he murmured
He drank more tea and then muttered,
'I wonder if they might consider adopting us.'"

POLISTINAE

One of two paper-wasp nests hanging from
Branches in our small farm dropped in the wind
And rain of the first storms of the fall season.
These wasps gather fibers from dead wood
And stems, and mixing them with wasp saliva and wasp
Blood, they construct cells and walls, living on nectar,
Caterpillars, flies, and beetle larvae. The combs of their cells
Look like a futuristic cityscape, something we
Might see in a wondrous movie about space travel,
Or the detailed aerial photographs of tin-towns
In a developing country, or even in one of our own
Tarp-and-cardboard-towns near a river.

PHILOSOPHER AND PERCH

The philosopher, carrying no water,
Picked up a gasping perch and took him along
To the fields, leaving the dry carriage rut
To a dusty snake who traded his skin for that
Of the red shadows moving in the road.
The perch spoke, "Philosopher,
Before you set me near the rice-field lock,
Where, as it drains into the stream, there
Will be plenty of water, please answer
One question, why do you bring books
With you when you travel?" The carriage
Wound through the countryside, creaking,
And the Philosopher answered, "So much
World shaking, my head aching with ideas,
I find the ancient words help me with my balance.
I have dropped countless cups of tea into
The puddles of modern life."

FIGURE A WAY TO SAVE THE WORLD

In *Cold Mountain, Hanshan* asks:
Do you have the poems of Han-shan in your house?
They're better for you than sutra-reading!
Write them out and paste them on a screen
Where you can glance them over from time to time.
So, with me, *Cold Mountain* on the bedside table,
Cold Mountain near the living-room recliner,
Cold Mountain in the office/guest room,
Cold Mountain on the kitchen table,
Cold Mountain in my back pocket,
Gleaned from used-book stalls and bins.
As the poet writes: *I use what remedy*
Is at hand to save the world.

TOO HOT OR TOO COLD

She wakes at 5:00 A.M. now, craving sunlight,
But she sleeps in her chair most of the day,
Calling me, if she gets too cold or too hot,
To help her get her sweatshirt on or off.
I open her front door as well as the window
Near her bed to let the ninety-degree heat
Come through her rooms. Still, she
Holds her arms around her as though
Cold. *While months and years flow by like*
A river, Hanshan says. Now, there are two
Wasps buzzing in the ceiling skylight box above her.

ALONG THE NARROW ROAD

Grateful for the gifts received along *the narrow road*,
For the *dumb luck, scrambled eggs and whiskey*,
Human wishes, spring rain and poppies, *or what you will*;
For a place to leave and rediscover on returning,
The long home, dream of the sky-land, hallelujah anyway . . .
Thoughtful *of gravity and angels*, and *imperfect thirst*, of a
Crow with no mouth, and *flower & hand*, and of the *mirror for the
Moon*, its *deep song, transformations, illuminations* . . .
Gratitude for our *night sky journeys: migrations: odysseys* –
The world doesn't end – and grateful for *the dead and the living*,
The wheel, one of innumerable wheels, up the *cold mountain*, and
Beyond the mountains, knowing this wheel of *life & death*,
Its *dream tigers*, its *hunger fields, howls*, or tolling *bells in winter*. . .
Respectful of our neighbors, let no one be a stranger to me.
And as I said at a poet's memorial, the reason words exist
Is to make each one of us a better human; or, as Bourdain said,
"If I'm an advocate for anything, it's to move. As far as you can,
As much as you can. Across the ocean, or simply across the river.
. . . walk in someone else's shoes or at least eat their food."

THE FOUR DIRECTIONS

Five miles outside the city limit, country roads
Bordered by vineyards, grasslands, oak-spotted hills,
Forested stretches along creeks and rivers,
A young, quiet family lives in a modest house
On one acre. Yesterday, their eight-year-old son,
Walking along the lane, pretended to shoot
His bow and arrow. Then he placed them on the ground,
Lifted half a set of antlers from his belt clip
And held them to his forehead, pointing them to each
Of the four directions.

DREAM

All through the dream I saw you,
The woman who helped me so many
Times, now a nurse caring for me in a vast,
Maze-like hospital. Fluids, medications,
Your calm and kind spirit. And, in my dream, as I
Left your care, I gave you a copy of *Cold
Mountain*. When I woke: your scent
And the scent of bone broth.

BEES IN THE SHIRLEY POPPIES

The area sprinkler hitting the acanthus leaves sounds
Like a spring stream hurrying along. Bees in abundance
Purr in the Shirley poppies. Hummingbirds rustle the
Nasturtium vines. Squirrels test the ripeness of plums.
This hermitage is kept beautiful with a little care each day,
A welcome respite from worldly worries. A few neighbors
Keep goats. One has two hogs, and several people raise
Chickens. Around here, there are no cows. The most
Abundant grazing animals are squirrels, moving through
The firs gleaning nuts from cones. Next, they'll be
In the quince, then on to the plums, or scurrying
Through the branches over the rooftop to the bird
Feeders to satisfy themselves with sunflower seeds,
Dropping some for a turkey peahen who has been
Expelled from the flock. Creatures, apart as all things
Are, yet connected by wind, seeds, song.

INHERITANCE

My mind is like the autumn moon, says Hanshan,
Shining clean and clear in the green pool. No,
That's not a good comparison. Tell me, How shall I explain?
I take up the question. Perhaps the cold
Of the mountain night affected your concentration.
Perhaps your mind is like the changing reflections
In the pool where the dragonfly flashes and flames
Across the surface – marking the impermanence
Of its quick life and its airy inheritance from sun's fire.

ACCOMMODATIONS

Ms. Gaunt ripped a wool blanket into strips,
Fashioned a noose, and hanged herself. "There's a failure
Of humanity here" said her son. "There were human
People looking after her who didn't care enough
To intervene when they saw such serious red flags.
It was obvious to any reasonable person that she was
In danger." Hanshan asks: *Have I a body or*
Have I none? Am I who I am or am I not?

TAHLEQUAH

"Flesh . . . rotted and . . . the spirit is fading away . . ."
Even after the body rots, regardless of what religious
Scriptures promise, finally, the Chinese believed,
The spirit fades into air. After more than three weeks,
The orca mother Tahlequah at last let her dead calf
Sink in the ocean. Perhaps the calf's spirit
Had finally faded from its body, and Tahlequah and her
Sisters had thereby completed their mourning.

THE MANY BIRDS

Cold Mountain said he lived farther away from others
Than he could describe – not the case with us here
In this rural area. Our street address is clearly posted
On our mailbox and gate. Near us in four directions,
We can count four towns, and a nearby highway is well-
Traveled. There is fog until noon in the summer, and hundreds
Of firs, oaks, madrone, pines, and cedar to hide our residence
From the road. But I am grateful that the hawks, eagles, owls,
Hummingbirds, woodpeckers, creepers, turkeys, swallows,
Oregon juncos, nuthatches, finches, orioles, flycatchers,
Chickadees, towhees, robins, vultures, ravens, crows,
Sparrows, egrets, herons, and geese know where we live.

WALKING FOR WHAT AILS US

Thinking of walking the Pacific Coast Trail,
Looking through the backpacker gear guide:
Lightweight Thinsulate puffy hoody: $200.
Trekking tights, close-fitting for performance: $175.
Thermo-moldable-synthetic hiking boots: $250.
Pack with suspension system, ribbed, belted: $300.
Packable food and tech gear, per month: $500.
Who knew? What an expensive proposition.
I'd better sleep on it, decide in the morning –
Summer, 6 A.M., hour of the raucous crows.
Marmalade-colored flowers bloom from broadleaf
Grasses. Hydrangeas below the firs need water.
Blessed, the miracle of birds in the trees,
The young in their nests call for sustenance –
I will walk here.

STRANGERS

Answering my daughter's call, I drive across town
To find her leaning against a wall,
A foil blanket wrapped around her shoulders.
Getting into the car, she says, "A woman came out of a sports store
And gave me this blanket." "How are you?" I ask.
She tells me that she has a friend who says she can see
My daughter's past lives and some dark energy chasing her.
"Centaurs, she calls them," she says. "Those half men/half beasts
Are your addictions," I tell her. She stares straight ahead,
Giving me directions. "Where are you going?" I ask.
Pointing at an RV, she says "Here." As she gets out of the car,
I see waiting yet another stranger.

TEA

Reverence for the art of tea, bowing to the room,
Its ceremony and ritual, bowing to the utensils,
The placement, measurements, the lines, being
Mindful to not show one's back to others, bowing
To the scroll, an artist's rendering of ever shifting
Life, its rift and sever, birth and resurgence, room
Within room, folded and refolded, bowing to the floral
Offering, ornament of the moment, the spirit of the tea,
Bowing to those near, revering the scent and sipping. Now
Reversing, bowing to every honored thing.
Ebbing and rising.

WHISPERS

An old man on the road whispers to the wind and the thin
Light coming through the leaves: *thistle turned to straw, red*
Leaves of the poison oak, blackberries ripe on abounding
Bushes, a black cat running to a hole in the fence,
A vulture shadow on the road, another creature well
Fostered by the sun as orange edges of maple emerge.
Wind moves the leaves, and, as they touch, there is a
Rustling sound and the scent of autumn.

MEMORY OF JAPAN

December has come – a hawk is calling, and its mate
Answers from a far-off fir. A towhee proclaims
The sunrise of the moment. I sit with my aged
Mother-in-law, as she sleeps, watching her breathing.
And I remember Michi and her floor-length hair.
Bamboo in the snow. Geese above bamboo. Brazier smoke.
That remote Japanese town, long ago, where I rode
A much too large bicycle amid small trucks and cars.
An old woman selling marbles through a fence – cat's eyes.

MOMENTS

Autumn's bright coolness – a three-trunked evergreen,
Needles and shadows, buttons of a green garment,
A robe filled with shadows. Afternoon sunlight –
Folded in her bedcovers, the old woman ignores
The birdcalls from her clock. *Tired . . . I just find life hard,*
She says. Autumn sunlight slants through trees, and
Finches flit at the feeders. The body once strong,
Rapid like a spring stream, running its course through
The years, now thin and shallow, murky, witheringly dry –
A pillar of gnats vanishes, autumn evening darkens.

LIGHT AND DARK

Leaves and needles falling in the winter wind. Winter moon,
Illumination so brilliant we take for granted the gravitational
Labor it pays to Mother Earth, and yet we praise its godly role
From its palace near the River of Heaven, mirroring the sun.
How do we lose our way with this much light? How is it
That so many can follow a man whose mind holds such darkness,
Driven by fascination with the grandiose and empire? Winter
Solstice, dusk in the towering firs. The golden tail of sunlight
Fleeing to the west, tail of sunlight flying to the Eight Islands.

GLORIOUS LEADER

Our Glorious Leader moves slowly,
His horns causing him trouble. He moves
Only to please himself, leaving a trail
Easily followed. One horn, *stupidity*, waves,
And so does his second horn, *provocation*.
He hails his base, demanding allegiance.
And he provokes much disagreement,
Purposely dividing his countrymen, and
He counters unity. See how the snail leaves its
Trail? Confusion, each horn vying for direction?

FLOWERING MAPLE

A yellow swallowtail butterfly turns seven times
Around the house, reverses direction seven times more,
Waiting for the hummingbird busy
Visiting each saffron-colored flower
Of the Chinese Lantern, a flowering maple –
What is the world telling me?
All of us have something we can't live without:
The nectar of a flower, the beauty of the world.

FATHER

There are great, mysterious words for the cancers
That affect the body – carcinomas, sarcomas,
Melanomas, lymphomas – when the normal growth
Processes of cells become uncontrollable.
It doesn't matter if a man knows the six arts,
Or possesses genius or riches or a generous heart.
Cancer can overtake him anywhere he is.
Father, Trouble was your middle name,
Chased in all four directions until you tumbled
To the earth.

SEEING MY DAUGHTER

Another tent-tarp-cardboard encampment
Against the fencing along the walk and bike trail.
When I come to see what drugs
Have done to my only daughter, I see sores
On her arms and hands, her face. Hanshan
Writes: *Life fades like a guttering lamp . . .*
This morning I face my lonely shadow.

WILD GEESE

Following the sun, which wanders but is not gone –
Rivers and mountains, the moon rising.
Red threads of the maple leaves.
An old man sighs. Pulling weeds, his back muscles strain,
Above him, mountainous clouds, and now he hears a hundred geese
Calling, and he stops to look. He lifts his hands to them
As they pass overhead, the fenced dogs silent.
He watches the geese fly, wanting to be flying with them.
Come in beauty, go in beauty, he thinks.

HAWK AND DOVE

Out walking, I see a gray feather on a gravel road,
And here a dove wing feather – ten paces more I spot
The short, black-striped and brown feather of a hawk,
Evidence of a battle in the air between
The tall firs that edge both sides of the road.
Two days ago I saw a flock of doves bolt
From the firs. All spring
I've been watching the nesting hawks, their
Fledglings crying for food.
And these feathers prove that a dove
Escaped or died trying.

MORNING WALK

Today, a farm girl, scrubbing out a horse trough, hears
Her dog barking at the sound of my feet on the gravel road,
And she turns to greet me, raises the brush, and we say
"Good morning" at the same time. She returns to scrubbing,
And I walk on, thinking of my ailing heart.
The medicines my doctor has prescribed make me weaker.
He recommends I give up wine! Perhaps I should drink
Root tea instead. Or take the boat that rows off with morning.

RAVENS, CROWS

Ravens, crows – my wife asks how to tell the difference.
One is the black sheep of the Corvidae family, but neither
Crosses the other. Ravens are larger, have a wider wingspan,
With pointed wings and tails, and quite the vocabulary.
Crows and ravens, never at a loss for voiced rebuttals.
And, my wife exclaims, a Native nation
Is named after crows, and look, here is a crow on
A scarecrow's shoulder!

NOTES

"Dragonfly and Woodcutter," page 1: This poem references Watson's translation No. 1, page 19.

"Not Given Much Thought," page 3: See Watson's translation No. 14 and his footnote regarding the polite arts.

"Philosopher and Perch," page 7: See Watson's translation No. 32 and his explanation of the tale told by the Chinese philosopher Chuang Tzu, who was asked for a dipper full of water.

"Figure a Way to Save the World," page 8: The quoted material at the beginning of this poem comes from Watson's translation No.100; the last line of the poem is from translation No. 94 and alludes to how Pineshadow uses the Watson translation as a remedy.

"Along the Narrow Road," page 10: In homage to the spirit and heart of Anthony Bourdain, 1956–2018, chef, observer, reader, writer, traveler. The italics in this poem are book titles.

"Inheritance," page 14: The Hanshan quote is from the Watson translation No. 97. In this poem, Pineshadow tries to answer Hanshan's question.

"Accommodations," page 15: The first quote is from Dane Shikman, speaking of his mother's suicide in jail on 8/2/15, as reported by Julie Johnson in *The Press Democrat*, June 19, 2018. In the second quote, found in Watson's translation No. 96, Hanshan ponders his death and imagines the fruit and wine that might be laid near his corpse.

"Tahlequah," page 16: See Watson's translation No. 90. The footnote reads, "According to Chinese belief, the spirit does not die immediately with the body, but only gradually fades away into nothing."

"The Many Birds," page 17: See Watson translation No. 46.

"Moments," page 23: The phrase "witheringly dry" is taken from Saigyō's waka, or short poem on page 47 in *Mirror for the Moon*. Saigyō, (1118–90) was born Norikiyo Sato. As a member of the Fujiwara family, he was of the samurai class. He resigned his duties at a very young age and became a wandering poet and recluse. Most of his writing is in the form of tanka, but like Bashō, his travel diaries are honored for showing respect for the arts of poetry, painting, and theater.

"Light and Dark," page 24: In line six, the phrase "a man whose mind" refers to Saigyō's waka on page 112 of *Awesome Nightfall*.

"Glorious Leader," page 25: I believe this image of the horns of a snail came to me either from Hanshan or Saigyō, though I cannot find it anywhere in my books.

"Flowering Maple," page 26: The abutilon plant is also known as the flowering maple, the Chinese bellflower, and the Chinese Lantern.

"Father," page 27: In line 6, "the six arts" is a reference to Watson's translation No. 14. His footnote explains that the six polite arts of the Chinese gentleman are etiquette, music, archery, charioteering, calligraphy, and mathematics. I have given him Trouble as a middle name, referring to the last line in No. 14: *His last name is Poor and his first name Trouble.*

"Seeing My Daughter," page 28: Pineshadow refers to Watson's translation No. 85, a poem that describes visiting relatives and the sadness about the demise of his family.

ACKNOWLEDGEMENTS

Many thanks to Lori Myers and Karin Phillips for their careful reading of and their astute comments on this manuscript. Thanks to Diane Frank, chief editor at Blue Light Press, for her editorial guidance. I am especially grateful for her forthright and passionate response to this book. My grateful acknowledgement of the debt owed to poet Carolyn Miller for sharing her generous editorial expertise which helped focus these poems, and for the design of *Walking Scarecrow*.

ABOUT THE AUTHOR

Mark Tate is the author of three previous books of poetry *Pommes de Terre* (2001), *Sur lie** (2002), and *Rooms and Doorways* (2003), and three novels, *Beside the River,* and its sequel *River's End* (McCaa Books, 2021), and *Butterfly on the Wheel* (McCaa Books, 2022). He served for ten years on the Sonoma County Poet Selection Committee for the poets laureate of that county. He is a long-time resident of Northern California where he lives with his wife, Lori.

www.ingramcontent.com/pod-product-compliance
Lightning Source LLC
Chambersburg PA
CBHW031217090426
42736CB00009B/959